Family
FUN

by Sadie Brumley

PEARSON

Glenview, Illinois • Boston, Massachusetts
Chandler, Arizona • Upper Saddle River, New Jersey

Who is in a family?

The people you love!

Mom is in a family.
Children are in a family.

Dad is in a family.
Dad reads to us.

Grandparents are in a family.

This family has a pet.

A family has fun!